Laura Ingalls
Wilder

Other titles in the Inventors and Creators series include:

Alexander Graham Bell
Milton Bradley
George Washington Carver
Roald Dahl
Walt Disney
Dr. Seuss
Thomas Edison
Albert Einstein
Henry Ford
Benjamin Franklin
The Brothers Grimm
Matt Groening
Jim Henson
Mozart
J.K. Rowling
Jonas Salk
Steven Spielberg
E.B. White
The Wright Brothers

Laura Ingalls
Wilder

Kaye Patchett

KIDHAVEN PRESS

An imprint of Thomson Gale, a part of The Thomson Corporation

THOMSON

~~*~~

GALE

Detroit • New York • San F   terville, Maine • London • Munich

LIBRARY OF CONGRESS CATALOGING-IN-PUBLICATION DATA

Patchett, Kaye.
  Laura Ingalls Wilder / by Kaye Patchett.
    p. cm. — (Inventors and creators)
  Includes bibliographical references and index.
  ISBN 0-7377-3159-1 (hard cover : alk. paper)
    1. Wilder, Laura Ingalls, 1867-1957—Juvenile literature. 2. Authors, American—20th century—Biography—Juvenile literature. 3. Women pioneers—United States—Biography—Juvenile literature. 4. Frontier and pioneer life—United States—Juvenile literature. 5. Children's stories—Authorship—Juvenile literature. I. Title. II. Series.
  PS3545.I342Z79 2005
  813'.52—dc22   2005013838

Contents

Introduction 6
  The Author of the Little House Books

Chapter One 8
  A Pioneer Girl

Chapter Two 15
  Hard Times

Chapter Three 23
  "Some Writing That Will Count"

Chapter Four 31
  A Much-Loved Writer

Notes 39
Glossary 41
For Further Exploration 42
Index 44
Picture Credits 48
About the Author 48

The Author of the Little House Books

L aura Ingalls Wilder was 65 years old before she started writing books for children. Her eight-book Little House series tells the story of her childhood as a member of a **pioneer** family in the American West.

Pioneers like the Ingalls family moved west to make new lives for themselves on the **frontier**. Laura and her sisters traveled west in a covered wagon with their parents, Charles and Caroline Ingalls. They journeyed hundreds of miles through dust, rocks, ravines, and waving prairie grass. Wherever they settled, Charles cut down trees and built a house with his own hands and farmed the untamed prairie land.

The United States changed in Wilder's lifetime. The west, once empty of white settlers, filled with automobiles, towns, and technology. Wilder decided to write down the stories of her pioneer childhood so they would not be forgotten. In the process, she became one of the world's best-loved children's authors.

The Little House books have been translated into over 40 languages, including Chinese and Japanese.

They have also been made into braille books for the blind. In her books, Wilder described what day-to-day life was like for pioneering families. Through her stories, Laura Ingalls Wilder has taught countless children and adults about the history of the frontier days. Wilder's books earned her many honors and awards, and they have sold more than 60 million copies worldwide.

By sharing her childhood experiences of growing up on the frontier, Laura Ingalls Wilder became a beloved author of children's books.

Chapter One

A Pioneer Girl

The baby girl who was born in the Big Woods near Pepin, Wisconsin, on February 7, 1867, had a long road to travel. Her name was Laura Elizabeth Ingalls. Before she turned thirteen, Laura traveled hundreds of miles in a covered wagon with her mother and father, Caroline Lake Quiner Ingalls and Charles Phillip Ingalls, and her sisters, Mary, Carrie, and Grace. They moved from Wisconsin to the Kansas prairie, where Pa built the little house that later became famous through Laura's books. After another stay in the Big Woods, they lived in Walnut Grove, Minnesota, and then in Iowa and De Smet, South Dakota.

People like the Ingalls family, who moved west to claim the lands on the western frontier, were called pioneers. In 1862, the government offered free land to anyone who could live on a **homestead** claim and farm it for five years.

Whenever more settlers arrived and new frontier towns grew, Charles Ingalls became restless and wanted to move farther west. Caroline wanted to settle near towns with schools that Laura and her sisters could attend, but

Charles and Caroline Ingalls moved Laura and her sisters to a little house on the Kansas prairie, which later became famous in her books.

Laura took after Charles. She did not care much for towns or crowds of people. She much preferred the wide, sweeping prairie lands and the wild things that lived on them. She and Charles would sing as the wagon traveled westward. Laura could always tell how Charles felt from the kind of music he played. "I *know* that Pa was happy," she said. "The fiddle music he played along the road west was rousing and rollicking."[1]

Frontier Childhood

Life on the frontier was hard. Food had to be hunted or grown. Charles built the family's houses and furniture himself, and Caroline made all of Laura's and her sisters' clothes. Laura had to help. She learned to sew—which she hated—and swept floors, made beds, collected chips for the fire, fetched the cow to be milked, and churned butter.

Although Laura's family was poor, her childhood was filled with songs, books, and poetry. In the evenings, Charles played his fiddle. He played hymns, sad Scottish tunes, and cheerful songs like "Yankee Doodle." He also told exciting stories about wild animals or funny tales of scrapes he got into during his own childhood. Charles's mother and Caroline's had both been schoolteachers, and Charles and Caroline both loved to read. They treasured their few books and often read them aloud. Stories and the rhythm of words were part of Laura's life.

A sign welcomes visitors to the Laura Ingalls Wilder museum in Walnut Grove, Minnesota, one of the places Laura lived as a child.

In 1874, after her family moved to a homestead claim near Walnut Grove, seven-year-old Laura memorized a poem that she loved from a Sunday school library book. It was called "Twenty Froggies Went to School." She would still remember it when she was an old lady.

Laura's imagination was always wide awake. Her lively mind took in all of the colors and movements of life on the prairie, from the jackrabbits, hawks, and gophers to the sweet violets and roses among the grasses. While Charles built houses and furniture, Laura was building memories.

School Days

In school, two of Laura's schoolmates, Nellie and Willie Owens, made fun of her for being a country girl. Half a century later, when Laura came to write the story of her school days, she would invent a character called Nellie Oleson, whose mean behavior would be based on those schoolyard memories.

Some memories were so sad that Laura did not want to remember them. In 1875, a baby brother, Charles Frederick, was born. Laura loved him, but when he was nine months old, Freddie got sick. "One awful day," said Laura, "he straightened out his little body and was dead."[2]

It was a bad time for the Ingalls family. Grasshoppers ate their crops, and in 1876 they moved to Burr Oak, Iowa, where Charles earned money helping friends run a hotel. Laura had happy memories of the Burr Oak School. She loved reading and writing, and she often won spelling bees against the whole school.

One teacher taught Laura and Mary how to read aloud. Laura learned how to make her voice sound excited or sad when she read stories or poems. The family lived over the town store, and Laura said, "Pa knew, but didn't tell us until later, that a crowd used to gather in the store beneath to hear us read."[3]

In 1878, the Ingalls family went back to their homestead, and Laura returned to Walnut Grove School. She enjoyed snowball fights, and she played baseball with the boys. She was proud that she could throw a ball faster than any boy in the school. "I was a regular little tomboy,"[4] she said.

Caring for Mary

Like all schoolchildren, Laura was sometimes sick. As a child, she had **malaria**, measles, and whooping cough. Doctors then did not understand what caused many diseases, and there were no shots to prevent illnesses.

In 1879, Mary fell ill. Pain stabbed her head, and she burned with fever. She was so hot that Caroline cut off all her beautiful, heavy hair to make her cooler. For a few dreadful days, the family was afraid she would not get well. Slowly, Mary recovered, but her eyes were weak. Soon, she went completely blind. Then Charles gave twelve-year-old Laura a special task. She must be Mary's eyes and describe everything she saw for her. Laura learned to describe things in such a colorful and interesting way that Mary told her, "You make pictures when you talk, Laura."[5]

Charles got a job with the railroad as a storekeeper, near the newly planned town of De Smet, South

A photograph shows the Ingalls family: Charles (front, center), Caroline (front, left), Laura (center, standing), and sisters Mary, Carrie, and Grace. Living on the frontier with limited resources meant that every member of the Ingalls family had to pitch in to provide food, clothing, and shelter.

Dakota. Laura described the whole journey to Mary as they traveled by train to join Charles. She described the sun slanting in through the windows, a red velvet hat, and a man's bald head. She was developing a talent for vivid description that would last a lifetime.

Growing Up

During Laura's first winter in De Smet, blizzards raged for seven months. To pass the time, Laura began to write poetry. She filled whole books. On the back of one, she wrote:

If you've read this book through
With all its jingles
I'll let you know that it's been filled,
By Laura E. Ingalls.[6]

Laura read her lesson books aloud for Mary. She helped more in the house, to give Caroline extra time with Mary. She was growing up. To help her parents save money to send Mary to a college for the blind, Laura waited tables in a hotel, babysat, and sewed twelve hours a day for $1.50 a week.

When she was fifteen, Laura earned her teacher's certificate. She did not want to teach, but it would earn more money. Her first teaching job was 12 miles (19km) away. She lived away from home and felt homesick and miserable.

A young homesteader named Almanzo Wilder took Laura home each weekend in his sleigh. Laura loved horses, and Almanzo—or Manly, as Laura called him—had the best horses in town. She enjoyed the rides and began to see Almanzo often. Caroline and Charles let Laura and Almanzo sit up in the front room until 11:00 at night. One stormy night, Laura fixed the clock so it would not strike the hour, so Almanzo could stay an hour later. Laura was grown up, but still mischievous. On August 25, 1885, she and Almanzo were married. Laura was 18 and Almanzo was 28.

Chapter Two

Hard Times

Laura and Almanzo Wilder lived on a homestead, in a house that Almanzo had built. At first, life was fun. Laura had her own horse, and she beat Almanzo when they raced across the prairie. She enjoyed working outdoors. On the farm, she drove the binder, which cut and tied sheaves of grain, pulled by six horses, and she tamed her own ponies to ride. More happiness came when she and Manly had a baby girl on December 5, 1886. Wilder named her Rose, after her favorite prairie flowers.

Then the Wilders' life darkened. Hail and drought killed all of the crops she and Almanzo planted. They watched helplessly as the grain they had sown with so much hope turned yellow and then dried up in the hot winds. In 1887, their barn and haystacks burned down. The next year, Laura and Almanzo were both sick with diphtheria. Afterward, a stroke left Almanzo disabled for life. For months he could hardly walk or use his hands.

Wilder's second baby, a boy born in 1889, died when he was just twelve days old. Two weeks later, a fire flared in Wilder's kitchen and burned the house to the ground. More crops died, and Wilder sewed to earn money. Most of the furniture was sold to pay debts. Laura and Almanzo considered moving to New Zealand.

Then a neighbor visited the Ozark Mountains, in southwestern Missouri. He returned with brochures that described the area as the "Land of the Big Red Apple" because of its flourishing orchards. He brought Wilder a huge, shiny red apple. Wilder set it on the windowsill. It seemed like a sign of a better life. In July 1894, she and Almanzo loaded their covered wagon and began the 650-mile (1,046-km) journey to the Ozarks.

Goodbye to Dakota

On the road to Missouri, Wilder a kept a journal. She described streams and valleys and the beautiful blue haze that covered the hillsides. She wrote nothing about how sad she felt—or how poor the family was. Wilder had cried when they left Dakota behind them. They owned nothing at all except for their wagon and team of horses and their few poor belongings, but in her journal Wilder made the trip sound like a happy adventure.

Wilder sent her colorful description of the journey to the *De Smet News*, which later printed it. It was the first story she ever had published.

She and Almanzo used all their savings—$100— to buy 40 acres (16ha) of rocky, hilly, ridge land covered in woods. On it were a log cabin with no windows and 4 acres (1.6ha) of young apple trees. They named their farm Rocky Ridge. Laura helped

Almanzo and Laura experienced some hard times as young homesteaders.

Almanzo saw down trees. They sold the wood, along with berries that they picked, to buy food. When the first load of wood earned 50 cents, Rose said that her mother "cried for joy."[7]

Moving Forward

Gradually, the Wilders cleared their land and planted more apple trees. At first, they lived in the town and worked while they built up their farm. Laura cooked meals for railroad men, and Almanzo had a hauling business and delivered oil.

Rose rode to school each day on her bad-tempered donkey, Spookendyke. Rose loved reading and was the best speller in the school. She brought home most of the books in the school library, and Laura, or Mama Bess, as Rose called her, read them aloud.

Wilder wrote often to Caroline and Charles to exchange family news. Then a message came from Caroline to say that Charles was dying. Wilder hurried

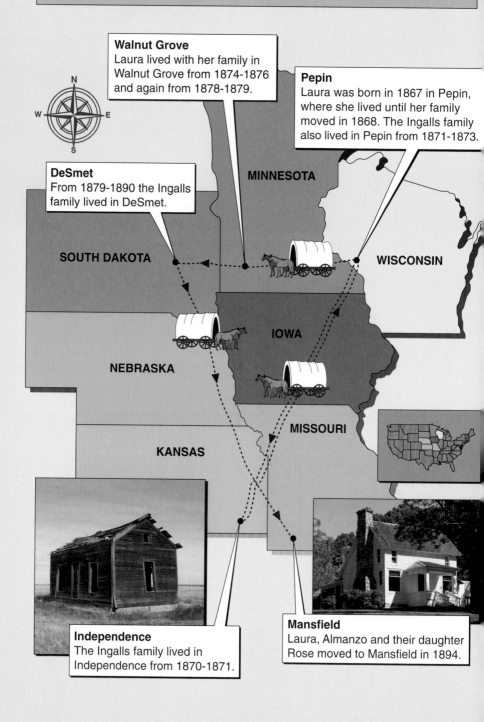

Laura's Travels

Laura Ingalls Wilder traveled to many places throughout her life. Her books were based on growing up in a pioneer family on the frontier.

Walnut Grove
Laura lived with her family in Walnut Grove from 1874-1876 and again from 1878-1879.

Pepin
Laura was born in 1867 in Pepin, where she lived until her family moved in 1868. The Ingalls family also lived in Pepin from 1871-1873.

DeSmet
From 1879-1890 the Ingalls family lived in DeSmet.

MINNESOTA

SOUTH DAKOTA

WISCONSIN

IOWA

NEBRASKA

MISSOURI

KANSAS

Independence
The Ingalls family lived in Independence from 1870-1871.

Mansfield
Laura, Almanzo and their daughter Rose moved to Mansfield in 1894.

Rose Wilder (right) and Laura roam the lands surrounding their home at Rocky Ridge in this photograph.

home by train. In the midst of her grief came a ray of happiness. Before he died, on June 8, 1902, Charles gave her his precious violin. "To think, Manly, he gave me the fiddle," Laura said to Almanzo. "It's the first thing I remember, Pa's playing us to sleep when we were little, in the Big Woods of Wisconsin. And by the campfires, all through that awful mud, across Kansas and Missouri. . . . We never could . . . have gotten through it all without Pa's fiddle."[8]

Rose remembered her grandfather's fiddle, too. He had played it just before they left for the Ozarks. She said, "It just lifted up the heart and filled it so full of happiness and pain and longing that it broke your heart open like a bud."[9]

Happier Days

Rose had inherited her grandfather's and her mother's love of music and stories. She was a good writer and a brilliant student. After she graduated from high school, she worked in Kansas City, first as a telegraph operator, and then as a writer for the *Kansas City Post*.

At Rocky Ridge, Laura and Almanzo were also doing well. Almanzo built a small house on the farm, and grassy meadows, grapevines, apples, pears, peaches, and fields of strawberries, oats, and wheat grew on

Wilder stands on the porch (inset) of the farmhouse at Rocky Ridge Farm, a house she designed herself.

what had been wilderness. Almanzo raised dairy cows, and Laura kept hens. Her chickens produced such good eggs that she was invited to give speeches about her methods at local farmers' meetings.

A Newspaper Writer

One day, a farm group asked Wilder to talk about her chicken farming. She could not be there, so she wrote out her speech and asked someone to read it for her. The **editor** of the *Missouri Ruralist* heard Wilder's speech. He thought it was so well written that he asked her to write about farm life for the newspaper. Wilder had written nothing before, except for letters home and her journal story when she had moved to the Ozarks. She said she would give it a try. Her first story for the *Ruralist* was about small farms. It was published on February 18, 1911, just after her 44th birthday.

In her next story, "The Story of Rocky Ridge Farm," Laura wrote about how she and Almanzo had turned a stony, tree-covered wasteland into a well-paying farm. She proudly told her readers that the farm had more than doubled in value after all the work she and Almanzo had put into it.

Rocky Ridge gave Wilder plenty to write about. That year, she and Almanzo started to enlarge their farmhouse. Laura designed the new house. It had ten rooms, lots of big windows, four porches, and a fireplace made with stones from the farm. When it was finished in 1912, neighbors said it was one of the prettiest houses in the Ozarks.

Wilder's newspaper stories were popular. She wrote a column called "The Farm Home," about fruit farming, chickens, and her farm neighbors. She became the *Ruralist's* household editor and later wrote another column called "As a Farm Woman Thinks."

Rose's writing career was moving forward rapidly as well. In 1914, she was hired as a reporter for the *San Francisco Bulletin*, and soon she was a successful writer. Rose gave her mother advice about her work and encouraged her to do more writing.

Chapter Three

"Some Writing That Will Count"

Laura visited Rose in San Francisco in 1915 to see the huge Panama-Pacific International Exposition. Some of the exhibits were about the state of Missouri, and Rose helped Laura write an article about them for the *Ruralist*. Rose gave Laura more confidence in her work. In a letter home, Laura told Almanzo, "I intend to try to do some writing that will count."[10]

When Wilder went home, she settled into her routine. As well as her newspaper work, she was very busy in the local town. She started clubs for farm women. They had discussion groups and raised money. Thanks to Wilder's fundraising efforts, the town got its first library.

For ten years, Wilder helped her neighbors and wrote about farm life in the Ozarks. She also had stories published in two national magazines—*McCall's* and *Country Gentleman*. Then in 1924, Caroline died. Wilder began to remember again the life she had led growing up as a little girl on the frontier. She thought how life had changed since then. Now she and Almanzo drove a car—a blue Buick that they called Isabelle—instead of a covered wagon. She realized

A poster advertises the 1915 Panama-Pacific International Exposition in San Francisco, which Wilder attended and wrote about.

that the pioneer days and the old family stories that Charles used to tell her were already a part of history.

Becoming an Author

Laura asked Rose, who was now a famous author, to write down Charles's stories so that they would not be forgotten. But Rose told her mother that she should write the stories herself. So, one day, Wilder sat down at her desk in her study at Rocky Ridge. She opened a school notebook with an orange cover, took up a pencil, and began to write. She wrote about her earliest memories, when she had lived in the Big Woods. "I went as far back in my memory as I could and left my mind there awhile," she said. "It would go farther back and still farther, bringing out of the dimness of the past things that were beyond my ordinary remembrance."[11]

Seen here in 1942, Rose Wilder, Laura's daughter, shared her mother's and grandfather's love of music and stories.

All of the people and places that Wilder had known long ago now crowded back into her mind and came to life on the lined pages. As she wrote, she was surprised to discover what an interesting life she had led.

At first, Wilder meant the book to be for adults, but a children's editor suggested that she rewrite it as a children's book. When the book was rewritten, Rose typed it and sent the **manuscript** to an editor at Harper and Row book publishers. The editor read it on the train on her way home. She was so interested in Wilder's story that she rode right past her stop. In 1932, when Wilder was 65, the book was published. It was titled *Little House in the Big Woods*.

"I did not expect much from the book," Wilder said, "but hoped that a few children might enjoy the stories I had loved."[12] Much to her surprise, her book was an instant success. She had not planned to write another, but children who read *Little House in the Big Woods* wrote and begged her to write more stories.

Writing Down the Past

Letters from children, librarians, and teachers all over the country filled Wilder's mailbox. She was delighted at their interest and decided to write a whole series of books for children. Her next book, called *Farmer Boy*, was about Almanzo's boyhood. Almanzo was pleased when children wrote letters to him. "He seems to have made quite a hit with the children,"[13] Wilder said.

Over the next ten years, Wilder wrote tirelessly. She wrote between washing dishes and doing chores. Sometimes she had an idea in the middle of the night.

Little House in the Big Woods, the first book in the Little House series, was published in 1932, when Wilder was 65.

When that happened, she would get out of bed and sit at her desk and write for hours.

Wilder tried to describe the scenes in her books so that her readers could see the pictures in their minds, just as she had described them for Mary long ago. While Wilder was writing *On the Banks of Plum Creek,* she gave a talk about her work for a local club. She told her audience: "There is a fascination in writing. . . . You will hardly believe the difference the use of one word rather than another will make until you begin to hunt for a word with just the right shade of meaning, just the right color for the picture you are painting with words. Had you thought that words have color? The only stupid thing about words is the spelling of them."[14]

Although all of her stories were true, Wilder changed some things when she wrote them. Her age in *Little House in the Big Woods* was two years older than her real age had been. When she described her family's life in the dugout beside Plum Creek, she said that the creek had a spring—but she confessed in a letter to Rose, "I have an awful suspicion that we drank plain

Although her family's home in De Smet was gone when Laura returned there in 1939, the home was eventually restored by the town and turned into a museum.

In her living room at Rocky Ridge, Laura Ingalls Wilder wrote her Little House books.

creek water."[15] One reader complained that she had not mentioned the name of a nearby town. Wilder apologized. She explained that she had not realized when she began to write the story of her childhood that she was writing history.

The "Land of Used-to-Be"

Before Wilder finished her books about South Dakota, she wanted to see De Smet again, to refresh her memory. In 1939, she and Almanzo decided to return for the Old Settlers Day celebration. "Early one morning," she said, "we packed our bags, put them in the trunk of the Chrysler, said goodbye to our pet bulldog and started to South Dakota and the Land of Used-to-Be."[16]

De Smet had changed since Wilder lived there. Fine brick businesses now stood along streets once dotted with wooden buildings. Laura and Almanzo went to visit the site of Charles's old claim shanty. The shanty was gone, but Wilder was glad to find that the cottonwood trees that Charles had planted were still there. Many people greeted Laura and Almanzo. "Everywhere we went we recognized faces," Wilder said, "but we were always surprised to find them old and gray like ourselves, instead of being young as in our memories."[17]

Wilder's trip to her old home reminded her of many more stories. She had planned to write three more books, but she had so many new ideas that she decided to write four more instead. Children wrote to Wilder all the time asking for more stories. They were eager to know how she met Almanzo and how they got married. "The children all seem wildly interested," Laura told Rose. "Lots of their letters want me to hurry up and write about it."[18] Every day she walked the half mile (0.8km) to her mailbox. She often received 50 letters a day and had to buy the biggest mailbox available, but she tried to answer every single letter.

In 1943, Wilder's last book, *These Happy Golden Years*, was published. She was 76. The book ended with her marriage to Almanzo. When children asked her why she did not write more books to tell what happened next, she said she wanted her books to end happily. If she wrote any more, she explained, she would have to include the sad things in her life. Just as she had done when she wrote about her journey to the Ozarks, she preferred to focus on happier memories.

Chapter Four

A Much-Loved Writer

Laura and Almanzo continued to live quietly at Rocky Ridge farmhouse. They listened to the radio, played cards, and read books. Laura did housework, cooked, and baked. Almanzo tended his goats and calves, worked in the garden, and tinkered in his workshop.

Although Wilder's way of life did not change, her books brought her many honors and awards. She was asked to speak at schools and on the radio. A special book award was created in her name, and several libraries were named after her. Five of her books were **Newbery Honor Books**. People who loved her books often stopped to visit at Rocky Ridge. Wilder showed them around and told stories about her family as they sat on the porch swing and listened.

In 1949, Almanzo died at the age of 92. He and Laura had been married for 64 years. Although she was lonely for Almanzo, Laura still had company. Children often knocked at the door wanting to meet her, and on her 84th birthday she received more than 1,000 cards and gifts.

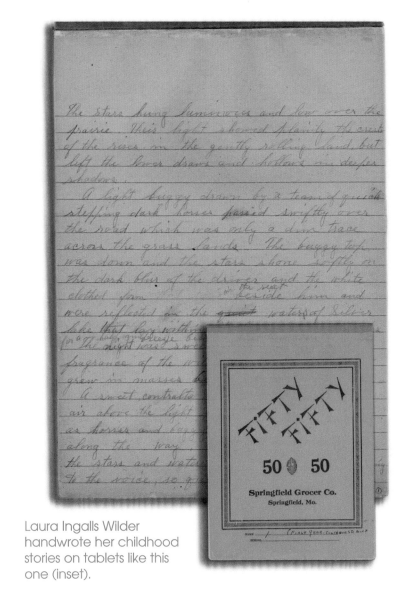

Laura Ingalls Wilder handwrote her childhood stories on tablets like this one (inset).

Each Wednesday, Wilder took a taxi into Mansfield to shop. She visited the library, which had a room named after her, and checked out mysteries and western books. On Sundays she went to church. She usually wore her favorite dark-red velvet dress with a lace collar and old-fashioned shoes with silver buckles.

"Mrs. Wilder was the prettiest old woman I ever saw,"[19] said Alvie Turner, who met Wilder when he was a boy.

When she was 87, Laura took her first trip in an airplane, to visit Rose in Danbury, Connecticut. The world was changed indeed since she had traveled the prairies in a covered wagon.

Bringing History to Life

When Wilder looked back on her life, she said, "I began to think what a wonderful childhood I had had .... I had seen the whole frontier, the woods, the Indian country of the great plains, the frontier towns, the building of railroads in wild, unsettled country, homesteading.... I realized that I had seen and lived it all. ... Then I understood that in my own life I represented a whole period of American History."[20]

Wilder's books were now in classrooms across the country, and she was delighted to know that she helped children learn to read. When they read Wilder's books, children found that history seemed to come alive. Students wrote and told her that they enjoyed learning from her books because her stories were about everyday things that happened to real people.

Wilder took extra care to research any details she could not remember. She made sure that experts checked all of the historical facts in her books before they were published. "In writing books that will be used in schools such things must be right,"[21] she said.

In later years, many modern readers were shocked at the way the *Little House* books referred to Native Americans as wild people who had no right to the land they lived on. Wilder grew up among homesteaders who did not understand the Native Americans' way of life and who believed that they were entitled to take land that Native Americans had already settled. In *Little House on the Prairie*, Charles told Laura that when white people came, the Indians had to move on farther west. Laura's reply showed her own sympathy. She asked whether the Indians felt angry when they were forced to move away from their land.

Caroline saw the Native Americans as wild and dangerous, and she was afraid of them. Laura was afraid her family could be harmed, but she was also very curious about the native peoples, and she understood and shared their love of the wide prairie lands. Later, after she had watched the destruction of an ancient culture as the Indians left the land forever, she described how empty and lonely the prairie seemed without them. As a child, she had not known that she and her family stood at a crossroads in the nation's history—or that her books would one day share the events that she had witnessed with millions of children around the world.

A Legend in Her Own Lifetime

Readers were interested in everything about the Ingalls family. Children and their parents visited the places where Laura's family had lived. In De Smet, local people showed visitors the buildings that were mentioned in Wilder's books and the location where the homestead had been.

When Wilder's hands became too stiff with arthritis to answer all her letters, she wrote a letter for her

Wilder (shown here at age 70) recognized the historical importance of her pioneer stories and was eager to share them with children around the world.

publishers to send to her fans. In it, she wrote a little about her life after the *Little House* books ended. She explained that Carrie, Grace, and Mary had all since died. She told of her friend Cap Garland's death while he was still young, when a threshing machine engine exploded, and how Nellie Owens, called Nellie Oleson in her books, got married and later died in Louisiana. "The 'Little House' Books are stories of long ago," Wilder said. "Today our way of living and our schools are much different; so many things have made living

Tourists examine Wilder's writing desk at the Mansfield, Missouri, museum where it is housed.

Today, Wilder's Rocky Ridge farmhouse is a museum, and it remains just as Laura Ingalls left it when she died in 1957.

and learning easier. But the real things haven't changed. It is still best to be honest and truthful; to make the most of what we have; to be happy with simple pleasures and to be cheerful and have courage when things go wrong."[22]

Laura's Legacy

On February 10, 1957, three days after her 90th birthday, Wilder died quietly at Rocky Ridge farmhouse.

Among Laura's papers, Rose found the diary her mother had written when she traveled in a wagon to the Ozarks. Rose added to the diary her own memories of the first years at Rocky Ridge and published it in 1962. She called the book. *On the Way Home.*

Rose also found another book among Laura's things. Like her other books, it was written in pencil, in an orange school tablet, but Wilder had kept it to herself. It told the story of the difficult years after Laura and Almanzo were first married. The book, *The First Four Years*, was published in 1971, two years after Rose died at the age of 81.

Rocky Ridge farmhouse was kept as a memorial to Wilder. Now called the Laura Ingalls Wilder Home and Museum, it remains just as Wilder left it. About 45,000 people come every year to see where Wilder lived and wrote her books. Among the exhibits is Charles's fiddle. Each year, during the annual Laura Ingalls Wilder Days, a musician takes the fiddle out and plays upon it all of the tunes that Laura loved back on the wide, windswept prairies of the Land of Used-to-Be.

Notes

Chapter One: A Pioneer Girl
1. Quoted in William Anderson, *Laura Ingalls Wilder: A Biography*. New York: HarperCollins, 1992, p. 75.
2. Quoted in Donald Zochert, *Laura: The Life of Laura Ingalls Wilder*. Chicago: Henry Regnery, 1976, p. 108.
3. Quoted in Zochert, *Laura*, p. 118.
4. Quoted in William Anderson, ed., *A Little House Sampler*. New York: HarperCollins, 1999 p. 8.
5. Quoted in Anderson, *A Little House Sampler*, p. 3.
6. Quoted in Anderson, *Laura Ingalls Wilder*, p. 112.

Chapter Two: Hard Times
7. Rose Wilder Lane, "An Autobiography," The Future of Freedom Foundation Web site. www.dahoudek.com/LIW/rosewilderlane.html.
8. Quoted in Anderson, *A Little House Sampler*, p. 68.
9. Quoted in Anderson, *A Little House Sampler*, p. 67.

Chapter Three: "Some Writing That Will Count"
10. Quoted in John E. Miller, *Becoming Laura Ingalls Wilder: The Woman Behind the Legend*. Columbia: University of Missouri Press, 1998, p. 126.
11. Quoted in Zochert, *Laura*, p. 234.
12. Quoted in Anderson, *A Little House Sampler*, p. 177.
13. Quoted in Anderson, *Laura Ingalls Wilder* p. 211.

14. Quoted in Janet Spaeth, *Laura Ingalls Wilder*, Boston: Twayne, 1987, p. 89.
15. Quoted in Miller, *Becoming Laura Ingalls Wilder*, p. 212.
16. Quoted in Zochert, *Laura*, p. 236.
17. Quoted in Zochert, *Laura*, p 238.
18. Quoted in Anderson, *Laura Ingalls Wilder*, pp. 203–204.

Chapter Four: A Much-Loved Writer

19. Quoted in Stephen W. Hines, *I Remember Laura*. Nashville, TN: Thomas Nelson, 1994, p. 212.
20. Quoted in Anderson, *A Little House Sampler*, p. 217.
21. Quoted in Anderson, *A Little House Sampler*, p. 179.
22. Laura Ingalls Wilder, "Laura Ingalls Wilder's Letter to Fans," Definitive Laura Ingalls Wilder & Little House on the Prairie Web site. www.laurasprairiehouse.com/research/lettertofans.html.

Glossary

editor: A person who works for a publisher and reads and corrects book manuscripts before they are published.

frontier: The farthest boundary of the settled area of the American West.

homestead: A piece of land that the government gave to anyone who would live on it and farm it for five years.

malaria: A disease that causes chills, fever, and sweating. Malaria is carried by mosquitoes.

manuscript: The pages on which an author writes a book before it is published.

Newbery Honor Books: The Newbery Award is an award given by the American Library Association for the best children's book of the year. Runners-up are called Newbery Honor Books.

pioneer: A person who went west to settle on frontier lands.

For Further Exploration

Books

William Anderson, *Prairie Girl: The Life of Laura Ingalls Wilder*. New York: HarperCollins, 2004. Tells the story of Laura Ingalls Wilder's life and the real adventures that inspired her to write the Little House books. The book also tells of Wilder's life after her marriage, and her career as a journalist and author.

Alexandra Wallner, *Laura Ingalls Wilder*. New York: Holiday House, 1997. A biography of Laura Ingalls Wilder, recounting her experiences as a member of a pioneer family. The book explains how she came to write the Little House books, and tells of her life in the Ozarks until her death at 90 years old.

Mae Woods, *Laura Ingalls Wilder*. Edina, MN: ABDO, 2000. A short biography of Laura Ingalls Wilder, describing Laura's life from childhood to old age, and her career as author of the Little House books.

Web Sites

Laura Ingalls Wilder, Frontier Girl (http://web pages.marshall.edu/~irbyl/laura/frames.html). Offers information about Laura, her family and friends, and a virtual tour of all the places where the Ingalls family lived. Visitors can also listen to some of the same tunes that Charles played on his fiddle.

Laura Ingalls Wilder Home & Museum (www. lauraingallswilderhome.com). The official Web site of Rocky Ridge, Laura Ingalls Wilder's former home, which is now a museum. The site offers information about the home and farm where Laura lived and wrote.

Index

awards, 31

Big Woods, Wisconsin, 8
birth, 8
Burr Oak, Iowa, 11

characteristics
    imagination, 11
    love of open spaces,
        9
    tomboy ways, 12
childhood, 10–14
Country Gentleman
    (magazine), 23

death, 37–38
De Smet, South Dakota,
    8, 13, 16, 29–30
De Smet News (news-
    paper), 16

education, 8–9, 11–12

fame, 36
Farmer Boy, 26
"Farm House, The," 21
farming
    in De Smet, 15–16

at Rocky Ridge,
    16–17, 20–22, 31
First Four Years, The, 38
frontier
    as history, 23–25
    homesteads on, 8
    life on, 10

Garland, Cap, 36

Harper and Row
    publishers, 26
health, 12, 15
homes
    childhood, 8, 12, 14
    in De Smet with
        Almanzo, 14–16
    Rocky Ridge, 17,
        20–21, 25, 31
homesteads, 8, 16
honors, 33

Ingalls, Caroline Lake
    Quiner (mother)
    characteristics of, 10
    death of, 23
    education of Laura
        and, 8–9

Native Americans
  and, 34
work of, 10
Ingalls, Carrie (sister), 8
Ingalls, Charles Frederick
  (brother), 11
Ingalls, Charles Phillip
  "Pa" (father)
  characteristics of, 8, 9,
    11
  death of, 19
  fiddle of, 9–10, 19, 38
  Native Americans
    and, 34
  stories of, 24–25
  work of, 9–10, 12
Ingalls, Grace (sister), 8
Ingalls, Mary (sister), 8,
  12–14
Isabelle (car), 23

jobs as girl, 14

Kansas City Post (news-
  paper), 20

"Land of the Big Red
  Apple," 16
  last years, 31–34,
    36–38
Laura Ingalls Wilder

Home and Museum, 38
legacy, 37–38
library, 23
Little House in the Big
  Woods, 26, 28
Little House on the
  Prairie, 34
Little House series
  Native Americans in,
    34
  Newberry Honors
    and, 31
  popularity of, 6–7, 26,
    31, 33, 34
  Rose and, 39
  writing of, 6, 26–29,
    30–31

Mama Bess, 17
marriage, 14, 38
McCall's (magazine), 23
Missouri Ruralist (news-
  paper), 21–22, 23
music, 9–10, 20, 38

Native Americans, 34
Newberry Honor Books,
  31

Old Settlers Day celebra-
  tion, 29

Oleson, Nellie (character in book), 11, 36
On the Banks of Plum Creek, 27
On the Way Home (Laura Ingalls Wilder and Rose Wilder), 38
Owens, Nellie, 11, 36
Owens, Willie, 11
Ozark Mountains, 16, 19, 21, 23

reading
importance of, 10
Rose and, 20
in school, 12
Rocky Ridge, 17, 20–21, 32

San Francisco, California, 22, 23
San Francisco Bulletin (newspaper), 22
Spookendyke, 17
"Story of Rocky Ridge Farm, The," 21

These Happy Golden Years, 30
Turner, Alvie, 33
"Twenty Froggies Went to School," 11

Walnut Grove, Minnesota, 8
Wilder, Almanzo "Manly"
book about boyhood of, 26
courtship and wedding with, 14–15
death of, 31
health of, 15
at Rocky Ridge, 16–17, 20–21, 31
trip to De Smet with, 29–30
Wilder, Laura Elizabeth Ingalls
on childhood, 11–12
on death of brother, 11
on importance of research, 33
on important values in life, 37–38
on letters from fans, 30
on Little House series, 26–27
on Pa, 19
on trip to De Smet, 29, 30
on writing, 23, 26, 29
Wilder, Rose (daughter)
birth of, 15

education of, 20
on Rocky Ridge, 19
as writer, 20, 23, 24,
   38
writings
   after Little House
      series, 36
   first published, 16
for magazines, 23
Mary and, 12, 14
for *Missouri Ruralist*,
   21, 23
poetry, 13
see also Little House
   series

Picture Credits

About the Author

Kaye Patchett has written four books for children. An award-winning freelance journalist, Ms. Patchett is also an editor and writes features for various Arizona publications. Originally British, she and her husband make their home in Tucson, Arizona, together with their shaggy dog, Fidget, and their cat, Fizzle.